W9-AOD-693

WITHDRAWN

Gramley Library
Salem College
Winston-Salem, NC 27108

COVENANT

Phoenix Poets

A SERIES EDITED BY ROBERT VON HALLBERG

ALAN SHAPIRO

COVENANT

THE UNIVERSITY OF CHICAGO PRESS

Chicago and London

Gramley Library
Salem College
Winston-Salem, NC 27108

Alan Shapiro, professor of English and creative writing at the University of North Carolina, Greensboro, is the author of three books of poetry. He was awarded the William Carlos Williams Award by the Poetry Society of America for Happy Hour, also published by the University of Chicago Press.

The University of Chicago Press, Chicago 60637
The University of Chicago Press, Ltd., London
© 1991 by The University of Chicago
All rights reserved. Published 1991
Printed in the United States of America

00 99 98 97 96 95 94 93 92 91   5 4 3 2 1

Library of Congress Cataloging-in-Publication Data

Shapiro, Alan, 1952–
    Covenant/Alan Shapiro.
        p.   cm.——(Phoenix poets)
    ISBN 0-226-75044-2 (cloth).——ISBN 0-226-75045-0 (pbk.)
    I. Title.   II. Series.
PS3569.H338C65   1991
811'.54—dc20   90-26379
                                                                    CIP

⊗The paper used in this publication meets the minimum requirements of the American National Standard for Information Sciences—Permanence of Paper for Printed Library Materials, ANSI Z39.48-1984.

For My Sister and Brother

Contents

Acknowledgments

Grateful acknowledgment to the following journals and magazines in which these poems or versions of them first appeared:

Agni Review "Sunday at the Dump," "At the Dump," "Marriage," "Home Movie"

American Poetry Review "Rock Pool," "Dawn Chorus," "Purgatory," "The Visitation," "The Sweepers"

Partisan Review "Turkey Vultures"

Poetry "Virgil's Descent," "Underground"

Threepenny Review "Cold Wood," "Dawn of Time," "Two Elegies," "Turn," "Separation of the Waters"

Tikkun "Love Poem"

Triquarterly (a publication of Northwestern University) "Night Watch," "Kinship," "Owl," "The Experiment," "The Lesson," "Maison des Jeunes," "Prayer on the Temple Steps," "Mud Dancing," "In the Kingdom of Pleasure"

Yale Review "Covenant," © Yale University

Also, I wish to thank the John Simon Guggenheim Memorial Foundation for a fellowship which enabled me to finish many of these poems.

one

The Sweepers

Who were they? The writer just calls them "sweepers," clearing
the streets, leveling a path for the army through the smoldering
debris of ancient houses torched and toppled all about them.
For six days, their heads bowed to the task, as they were told,
nameless, stateless, were they slaves, now serving other masters,
having already learned this lesson, neither saddened nor relieved
that the rooms they served in were now rubble to be pushed aside?
Or that their masters lay there crushed among the stones
and timbers, some of them still wailing, calling out for mercy
as they shoved and turned them over, old hands at going on?
Or were these the masters? the wealthiest? their money,
somehow, having gotten them this far, as yet unharmed?
their fingers blistering as they plied crowbar and boat hook,
dowel and axe, the pain a punishment for the dumb animal
persistence that so easily and thoroughly turned friend and relation,
the whole rich tapestry of customary feeling, law, memory and lore
into mere fill for gullies?—Did they resent the half-dead
for their clumsy fit, their ineffectual resistances,
the ones stuffed head down, legs above the surface
writhing pathetically to get away, like giant insects,
or the ones feet first, their heads above the surface
unable even to flinch as the horses trampled over face and skull?

The writer doesn't say. For a few lines in my Roman history,
for six days and nights, nameless, stateless, ever diligent
they clear the streets, they make the way smooth for Scipio,
who, it is said, was weeping, sunk in thought, as he looked on,
weeping at the fortunes of cities, peoples, empires:
the Assyrians had fallen, and the Medes, and the Persians
after them had fallen, and so too, latest of all,
latest and most brilliant, the Macedonians blotted out,
destroyed, as Ilion had been destroyed, and Priam,
and the people of Priam of the strong ash spear . . .

Here one turns the page, and goes on reading.

Maison des Jeunes

"Nuit sans étoiles, nuit obscure"
—Baudelaire

After the woman I was visiting had gone in to bed
some nights I would see a woman undress on a balcony.
The long playground below us, which our buildings fronted,
would already be deserted by everyone but the men
at their game of boules far at the other end. Their pitch,
the only strip of dull light cut in the darkness
made duller by the slow twining of cigar smoke
over and around them, the quiet made more quiet
by the random click of the balls, by the laugh or groan
that would rise for a moment above the constant
murmuring and then fall back.

                                    All through the twilight
I would look out toward her building and never know,
for certain, who she was among the countless mothers
on balcony after balcony hanging up and taking down the day's
        wash.
The same clothes always in different places, a sluggish
eddying of orange and blue, white, pink or olive
blouses, pants, slips, socks and dresses up and down
each bleak facade. Her voice, somewhere among the voices,

would have been calling from time to time down to the playground
loud with children, a mesh of excited cries, shrill bits of
            singing,
from which each magnetic call, weary or cross, or both,
would pull in one reluctant child, and then another.
When the dark thickened, always the same two remained:
a fat boy dribbling a soccer ball in one place
fluidly from knee to knee to forehead back to knee,
while a friend bicycled around him, veering as close
as he could to swipe the ball away, and always missing,
because the boy, clairvoyant in his own finesse,
would take one half-step back or forward, shift the ball
so tauntingly beyond the other's reach the other,
jittery with hope, would have to go on playing.

                                Each night
the longer she would keep me waiting, the more unexpected
was her white shirt's fluorescent glow against the dark,
down which her vague hand moved from button, I imagined,
down to button until her shoulders arching back
a little let the loose shirt slip as smoothly as water
down her bare arms. Her dark skin now so merged with darkness
that the sudden black flare of breast was like a gift
the late hour gave and took away, so as to urge from me a more
intense stare that would later make her memory keener than sense.
Maybe her husband was among the men she could have watched
passing in and out of small groups now, to and from their turns,
a bottle drifting languidly from hand to hand; slower
and slower, as though to prolong each other's reverie
of these after hours, postponing each waiting bed,

each getting up tomorrow. Maybe she could have heard
her husband among their voices, the seamy, intimate, male
exchange of secrets they (their scant wages already portioned to
            their wives)
had earned the right to keep. If only one of them had seen her
she would have been another secret in the smoke-slurred
light of their little freedoms; she would have been in his mind,
later, as he lay down beside his wife.

                                    As I lay down,
she was the woman I would need to wake, those nights,
waking my friend. Hers, the darkness that would open up for me,
draw me down deeper, and never deep enough. Beyond me, always,
the promise of her unseeable face, the mild dreamy argot
of her moaning what could have almost been a name.

At the Dump

1. Sunday

From the station wagon on the shoulder of the road
before the junkyard, Brother Paul, the radio preacher,
is pouring out "the sincere milk of the Word" as I pull in.
The voice is a mustering hosanna, roiling onward and upward
through the noon air thick with heat about the blessings
of the ever-offered hand of the savior, and what it is
that keeps our sad hearts clenched like a fist against it . . .

They must have come straight from church, for the man there
rummaging through a dumpster is dressed up in a brown suit
and burgundy tie, and the little girl behind him
holding her own hands is staring down helpless and unhappy
at her bright black shoes already dulling in the dust haze
her father kicks up as he heaves aside bald tires, cartons, bags.
Neither of them turns as I drag the dented basin from the car.

Nor does the man notice, nor care, that sweat streams crookedly
down his face and neck, into the tight white collar,
darkening his tie, his mind fixed only on the plastic sack
he wrestles up from the heap with one hand while the other

jimmies the brass rod poking through it back and forth
till it slides free, and a wet mulch of rinds, meat scraps
and cans falls away across his arm, flecking the coat and cuff.

But the rod's bent, one half dangling from the other.
He gestures as if to hurl it down, but stops himself
at the last moment, and lets it drop. He sags back, eyes closed,
lips trying to keep pace with the preacher's quivering twang,
"Eye on the sparrow, eye on me," but it's too hot, the air
too littered with flies, and he is only Adam's son now
drawing a soiled sleeve across his brow to mop the sweat away.

Now the preacher's voice seems to rise on the white wings
of its own rejoicing beyond the dumpsters, through the scraggly
        pines,
and out across the bright widening swath of the half-constructed
        highway
"to that place the unredeemed call heaven, but the saints call
        home."
When I reach the car the girl is tugging lightly on his sleeve,
and like a child wakened too suddenly, dazed, he follows her
to the basin tilted upside down high on a mound of trash.

He eases it off, then waits, holding the handle at one end
while the girl grips the other with a single hand, so her free
        hand
can press the pink frills of her dress against herself
away from the rusted blessing, as if these were the last new
        things
on earth, and all she can do to protect them, to keep them clean,
is pause, readjust her grip, and as she lifts it let her thin
arm tremble, her eyes clench with the might of so much prayer.

2. Saturday

He would have to want her, if he would just open his eyes.
Want her and be stung by how utterly she couldn't care
whether he wanted her or not. His aging wild thing turned
half toward him, half away, with one hand on the dumpster
and the other running slowly across the big haunch
her tight jeans pock and ripple, almost fondling herself
the way his hand would, if she would let it. Just look,
she seems to say, I dare you, even here, even now,
even despite the ratty orange tank top, the nose plugs,
the plastic shower cap keeping the trash out of her hair.
He, though, isn't just leaning the shiftless buddha of himself
against the pickup, walkman in hand, eyes closed, head nodding,
but resisting, his loafing bulk warding her off
as that buttonless hawaiian shirt pulled back like curtains
makes the black two-headed serpent whirl from his navel, at her,

then away, up over the wide repose of belly, to the chest
where the left head curling right and the right left lock,
stretch and undulate into YOU MOTHER, to finish at the nipples
around which both fanged jaws, dripping, have opened wide.
So slyly at ease that his slack lips singing, yeah yeah
com-a-com-com-a-com-a, his faintly trilled falsetto, is all it
          takes
to make her see how this doing nothing wouldn't be the kick
it is if she weren't working in front of him to witness it.
Their blind boy off to the side, slumped over the arm of a
     couch,
bare knees on the gravel, is lost in the contemplation of his
          hands
as they pull out clumps of batting from the gashed cushion,
pawing the coarse stuff, parsing it down eagerly to strands,

the strands to nothing. The busier his fingers, the more
the sounds surrounding him must blur and run together
till the dark cloth of the air is nearly patternless.

Now, though the woman has bent over the dumpster
and begun to rail, I've a right mind, god damn it, a right mind,
all the boy hears is the muffled clang of bottle, trash
washing away, dissolving. Even when she yells in his face
every scavenged good—bent fork, shredded blouse, a shoe:
each just another piece of evidence, it's an open and shut case,
she never gets anything but fooled—all he does is tilt
his head a little closer to the cushion now in his hands.
All he needs to do is cock his ear, run his listening down
along the seam and fringe, over the crooked mouth of the tear,
then begin to urge it apart so gently, so tenderly attentive,
that it is the fabric now which seems to move his hands,
his hands become its will, the longing in the mesh to loosen,
fray and unravel into these delicate soft hairs and softer
filaments tumbling one after another from his fingers.

If he could see it he would think how giddily it yields
to its own lush wrecking, with what exuberance, like snow
in water, as surely as a sound, it vanishes down
the glinting screes, the ever diminishing ever shifting
passages of gutted sacs, crushed cans, newsprint, rags and wire.
And he would wave to the other two, the lovers, to come see,
come see how eager it is to be rid of being ours.
But his hands are hungry, pawing each other now for one last
thing to pull apart. And as he lifts his blank gaze he can only
feel himself stitched back into the coarse dull webbing,
the fervorless resiliencies that lock the lovers just where they
        are:
the woman whispering honey, hon, as she draws one finger, one
sharp nail, ever so slightly down through the tangling

Gramley Library
Salem College
Winston-Salem, NC 27108

black letters of the serpent, and the man, all will,
still singing as he struggles not to open his eyes.

3. If I Were There

Last night in the dream I woke to hear you weeping,
weeping downstairs some hoarded grief. At my least
stirring to come down to ask you what it was, it stopped.
You quieted, not to be caught, not to have me even
near that inwound privacy. And I admit I thought
(not because you wanted this), she's calm, it's all right now,
and fell asleep, only to be again awakened.
                                                        Believe me,
if I were there, I would waken when your sleep
breaks, as it does these nights; I would see you
a bewildered sentry, staring off in darkness, at darkness,
trying to see what wants you there awake.
If I were there, you would hear me speak. My voice
would come so gently through the quiet it would seem,
at first, the quiet given tongue, the quiet dreaming
what I say, the slow unwinding rhythm of it
in my hand drawn over and over through your hair . . .

That woman at the dump, the scavenger, remember—
broad-shouldered, bare-armed, grimed and sweaty,
the plywood she had roughed up from the garbage
under one arm, remember how she passed the blind boy
holding her other hand behind her, palm up,
straight out, never looking back, and what was strange,
remember, was how he didn't wait for her to speak,
or touch him, or even pause, but raised his hand then
at that footstep, in that distinctly ruffled air,

his hand held only toward hers, near but not in it,
as if the touch's aura made it possible for him
to rise, to move as she did deftly in that complicated
swerving past the baling-wire spools, the black
tubes snaking in the grass, the shattered bottles.
How she got him through the treacherous debris was simply
how the day ended, like any day. Like this one. Like this.

The Visitation

Up on the right an old guy honking, honking,
as car after car lurched past him toward the jammed light
where other cars honked through the intersection, inching forward
from all directions in a tight knot they were trying to untie
by tying tighter, till it was my turn not to let him through.

Hatred banging on the wheel, hatred freshening
the grizzled face bent toward me, explaining, fuck you, pal,
fuck you! Sweet hatred making it my fault he had to lunge out
before me, that my brakes slammed, that I yelled back, asshole,
what's the rush? The good solace of it mine now as he passed.

And as someone else leaned hard on the horn to edge me on,
I thought of angels, how when they come among us in disguise
it's here they find us—stuck in each other's way,
feet on the pedal, burning, burning
to go forward before someone else cuts through.

Mud Dancing

—Woodstock, 1969

Anonymous as steam, in the steam teased
from the mud-hole at the field's edge
where we were gathered, the unhallowed dead,

the herded up, the poured out like water,
grew curious about us—naked as they were
once, our numbers so like theirs,

and the air, too, a familiar newsreel
dusk of rain all afternoon.
It could almost have been themselves

they saw, except that we were dancing
knee deep in mud, in the muddy
gestures of their degradation,

unpoliced and under no one's orders
but the wiry twang and thump
we danced to, sang to, yowling

on all fours, hooting on backs and bellies,
smearing black lather over our own,
each other's face, arms, hip

and crotch till we were sexless, placeless,
the whole damp mesh of who we were that made us
strangers to each other, the shalts and shalt

nots of you and me, mine and not yours,
cast off easily as clothing
into the blurred shapes of a single fluency.

Was this some new phase of their affliction?
The effect of yet some new device—
to make them go on dreaming, even now,

some version of themselves so long accustomed
to their torment that they confused
torment with exaltation, mud with light?

Frau History, they asked, *is this the final
reaving of what we loved well, that we should
swarm now in the steam over the indistinguishable*

*garments scattered everywhere in piles, that
we should need, even now, to sort through them,
to try to lift in our vaporous hands*

*the immovable rough granite
of this sleeve or collar, that vest,
those sandals, the flimsiest top?*

Virgil's Descent

Not Moses but another Tantalus—
to have been granted this much, and no more,
to see beyond the stream he'd never cross,

near but no nearer now, on the far shore
those hymning veils impenetrably bright
about the gift he was not chosen for.

His only grace there on that blessed height,
as he turns back, would be another chance
to climb down like a body from the light

slowly enough to see its radiance
shine dim and dimmer in the rising eyes
he sinks past, past their lightening penitence,

down through the fire that scorches till he dies
of being unsinged in that weightless flesh
each step leads further now from Paradise.

Upward forever, the flayed gluttons, whores,
killers and con men to their just reward,
all jostling by him in a holy mesh,

each soul a syllable within the Word
he'll study, and repeat, and never master
century after century . . . Now they deboard:

the naked cargo of a new disaster,
women and children, Gypsy, Slav and Jew,
their charred flesh smoking out of every boxcar,

eerily in the steam they wade out through,
down the long platform, shivering, half-afraid
they're not arriving but returning to.

They hurry off, they scramble in the prayed-
for dark, away from the wandering aura where,
never more hopeless, never less assuaged,

he sings, he sings about the burning sphere
of love not meant for them, whose burning fueled
another kind of transport straight to here.

The more he sings, the more the song seems cruel,
and more mysterious —the merciful
bright manna now an ash of syllables

he can't not sing, the more they fade and swirl
endlessly in and out of one another
over the floor of that vast terminal

the way birds at a sudden shot will scatter
to far trees, and still farther, as if they
could hear the sharp blast echoing forever,

and nowhere could be far enough away.

t w o

Night Watch

He pauses where the road crests,
and somewhere deep in the woods
a dog rouses; the faint
howling so far up back
behind the trees it seems
to come unplaceably
from all directions, more
the nimbus of a sound,
he thinks, than sound,
what the stars would be
as voices as they slant down
the steep night into the massing
thicker night of trees
below him, each one howling
its colossal earth-dwarfing
fire over light-years
of light-years to this
speck-like brushing in his ear.

Who was it? What was his name?
More than a thousand miles from here
and over thirty years ago,
who was the boy who told him—
one night behind the school,
in the alley where the older boys
like cavemen huddled round a fire
were playing cards, by matchlight—
that everything anybody
ever said on earth had to
rise through the night sky
and say itself forever
to the stars, and past them;
every wisecrack, or lie,
even the soft slap of card
on pavement, the clinking coins,
the terse nova of each struck match,
fading forever but never faded
as they rose; and that some day
he would invent a radio
so powerful it would gather up
his voice last week, last year,
the first word he ever spoke,
and transmit it back
through the crackling
interstellar airwaves?

Even now up past the Dog Star
he would be saying
that boy's name as they parted,
as he always did, as if
he would always say it,

as if each time didn't bring him
closer to the year
or two, or more, when he would
say it for the last time
here on earth—saying it
again beyond the Dog Star,
the North Star, Bear and Archer
in a voice he wouldn't recognize
if he heard it now.

The Experiment

His mind is keen with relations,
studying the way the lamplight
slanting down at 45 degrees
across his mother reading on the couch
illuminates one half of her face
by darkening the other, and beyond her
to his left, her right, how it cuts
diagonally through his subject,
"the baby," as she still calls it,
who squealing mine! mine!, its one
and only word, has just waddled
through the carefully positioned
phalanx of soldiers and knocked them over,
sweeping them aside to get to the tank,
the artillery gun, the bombers, each piece
thrust in its mouth and hurled away
as though a baby's toy, and not
the free world's last defense.

It no longer now concerns him
whether or not she stops reading.
For he has factored both contingencies
into the plan, stationing himself
and the subject north by northeast
so that even if she does look up
their two backs is all she will see.
She will have to think how nice it is
the two boys get along so well
when, just as expected, the subject
giggles as he rubs all over
its forearm the cool thick glaze
of the lighter fluid he has secretly
requisitioned from the pantry
and which, according to his calculations,
if evenly applied, should burn
exactly six seconds before she notices
it singeing even a single hair.

He steps back, holds the small wrist out,
and saying, this is just a test,
I repeat, this is just a test,
touches the match head to it.
The room suddenly wild with data:
at six one thousand flame gusts
up the arm the subject's waving
like a new toy, crying mine! mine!
so gleefully that at five one thousand
his mother laughs, what are you sillies doing,
still smiling at four, though leaning forward
beyond the lamplight, till at three,

her face now wholly dark, it's
what are you crazy?, throwing her shawl
down over the subject who at two,
not one, is deliriously crying
as she rolls the smoking bundle of him
backward and forward on the floor.

At two, not one. A thinner solution
at the same distance, or the same one
farther away, could—he is certain—
cut it closer. Though how thin? how far?
Now the baby swaddled in her lap,
face phlegmy with tears, still whimpering,
has picked up the F-14 and is
sucking on it while she strokes
the not even barely singed arm.
Does he know he could have killed him?
Does he? Can't they be friends? Like friends?
What she has failed to understand
is how that would fall outside his
already wobbly perimeters of defense,
and competence. This is a problem
strictly of logistics, proximities,
angles of vision. And no, no,
he isn't crazy. Only curious.

The Dawn of Time

Because the hallway between
the kitchen and the den holds
midnight in the middle of the day,

I know the clouds have darkened
outside to the same sky as
in my book, *The Dawn of Time:*

the same close cave-gray covering
above the vast gray field where
you could see, far in the distance,

herd after herd of caribou,
bison and elk, immense antlers
tangled against the skyline

like a migrant forest. And closer,
in the middle distance, deer,
coons and smaller creatures

forage together in a great calm,
mindful of flower, leaf and stem,
while others near them, others of their kin,

scatter away before the slashing
saber-tooth tiger that would soon,
tidily, perish from the earth.

In the foreground, the woolly mastodon—
bigger than a house though half-sunk
to his stomach in a black pit—

rears his astounding tusks at the tiny
furry hunters who surround him
hurling their pin-like spears.

Off in the right-hand margin, too,
halfway uphill within a cave
before a little fire—someone

is scratching the same kill
across the cavewall, while beyond
the great ice sheets inch forward . . .

The doorway to the kitchen frames
nothing of my mother but her hands
on the white table, one hand

filing the other's nails while
at the hallway's other end
blue and pale blue shadows

throb and eddy through the dark
den where my father dozes
on the couch before the television.

Evolution, the teacher told us,
is everything that happened
since the dawn of time

that made it possible
for us to learn about it.
It is, she said, a great

continual migration
and where we are is only
where it's gotten to today.

Each sharp nail catching
the kitchen light above it
like a chip of fire

as the file goes over
in short bursts back
and forth, back and forth,

and each time faster as if
to make the nails flare
up with hidden power;

dream signals from the den,
a liquid mingling of grunts,
calls, words and wordlessness—

the two sounds, file and dream,
kitchen and den,
held in my hearing

in the hallway where it's
even later than it is,
sky of the Ice Age,

same sky under which
whatever we are is only
where we've gotten to today.

Cold Wood

—for Simone

One night I heard my parents calling
my name out softly through the dark house;
their voices nothing but a mild
greeting I didn't know I longed for

till I heard it, so far away
in the quiet that the sheets
I slid from and my softest step
were loud enough to make it vanish

from me as it drew me on, from bed
to hall, to landing, halfway
downstairs to where the bannister
between floors straightened before

descending toward their room. I paused,
my hand cold on the slippery wood.
Their calling still too far, too fugitive
to be down there. And it came to me

they must have flown up through the stairwell,
beyond the window, to the tree
where the leaves shivered the streetlights
into branching stars and tangling comet trails

whose shadows slid down the wall
over the bannister and through my hand.
Yes, they had dreamed themselves up there—
to sing my name, birds in the heaven-tree.

But my hand was heavy on the cold wood.
And the whole house heavy with listening
was falling away from the twined stars
shrinking to the wavering edge of sight

and then beyond it, till all of the night,
the black orient spaces were between me
and their voices, which were now just the trace
of voices, the trace of my happy name.

The Lesson

For a long time afterward
all I could think of
was the one time
he took me: the slow
ride back, him saying,
see, like this,
his fingers claw-like
against the wheel,
like this, with the seams,
let's see you do it,
now snap it down hard
this way, that's right,
that's the fuckyknuckle.
And he smiled then as if
he saw ahead of him
all the things I'd do
with what he showed me.
I remember thinking that
if people on the street
had seen the pebbly
gold sheen of the car
among the ordinary
traffic, if they had seen

him talking, smiling
when I held my hand up
claw-like, just like his,
they would have thought
he was a proud father,
I was a lucky son.
How would I ever say
to anyone who he was?

I was ten that summer,
and I loved Rich
with a keen aimlessness
I couldn't name, or hide,
or not let draw me
to the playground every day
to wait for him, to wait
there, restless and sullen,
with a few friends
who were nothing more
to me but glum
reminders of what I was
without him, what I
couldn't be till he arrived.
It didn't matter that
I knew he came just
after one each day—
I still tried
to convince myself
each moment he didn't show
was just proof he wouldn't.
I tried to work myself up
into utter hopelessness
so I would feel—when the gold
Sting Ray came round the corner—

how suddenly waiting
could be not waiting now,
not having having.

And what I had, then,
was an almost holy
feeling of unworthiness
that he would come
at all: Rich
all the more mysterious
for looking just like
anybody's father
in a brown suit, tie
he never loosened.

How's it hanging?
he'd ask us from the center
of the chrome-lined golden
nimbus we couldn't keep
from touching, drawing
our hands over the sloped
sides, the grooves and channels,
and the sleek wedging
where the headlights hid.
The whole car radiant
with everywhere he'd been,
everything he'd done.

How's it hanging, boys?
he'd ask, and tap
the wheel, jiggle the stick,
the engine revving

gently, not so gently,
to remind us of all
the other things
he could be doing.

Were we Little Leaguers?
Did we want to learn
a cool pitch no one
else knew how to throw?
It was a combination
screwball/knuckleball
he called a fuckyknuckle.
And he would teach it
to each one of us. Promise.
And we'd never lose.

So how could we not
want to please him
when he'd ask if
anyone could tell him
what pussy was,
slit, gash, hole?
What made hair
grow on our palms?
What did it mean to
dip the wick? To bugger?
Bang? Ball?

            And what
seemed to please him
most was how we giggled.
Giggled because we knew
the words were power
without quite knowing

what the power's for.
He liked to see us struggle
not to look away;
he'd smile, then,
without derision, awkwardly,
his eyes just a little
bit averted, as if
our high-pitched ignorant
unease aroused some
unease in himself,
as if the words so
casually uttered in his
deep voice, then repeated
skittishly in ours,
had brought us both
to the edge of some
forbidden place, or,
rather, to two
forbidden places—his place
for us, ours for him.

Then the rides had started.
Each day, he'd want to know
who's hanging longest?
and before we could answer
he'd pick just one of us.
Each day it wasn't me
I'd watch them vanish
round the corner and
imagine as they shot down
avenue and boulevard
how the speed would be
its own green light
through all the intricate

traffic-guiding grammar
of signs and signals, the two
of them a bright blur
past the marveling neighbors,
past the houses, schools,
out beyond the city
to a blessed grove
of going even faster.

When they returned, the boy
would never say
what happened, where they went.
Aloof now, troubled,
it seemed, by being
back among us, he would move
in what I took to be
an otherworldly charm,
a secrecy
of having been beyond
anything we knew
or had words for,
but Rich's words. That's why,
I thought, nothing
was ever said, and why
from then on he didn't
stammer, as we did,
or blush, or stand there
scolded when Rich chose
another boy, and still
another to go off with him.

Till, Hey, stop pulling your pud
and get in, he said
one day, and suddenly
all the complex multi-
colored gauges were
before me, their arrows
trembling up
eagerly for the speed
Rich held back as we
crawled down side street
onto side street.
Where were we going?

Hey, had I seen
the Dick Stick?
From the glove compartment
he pulled out a rubber
penis that fit
over the stick.
And shifting from first
to second, back to
first again, he
stroked the grotesque
veiny sides of it,
tickled the big head
and chuckled to see me
chuckle nervously.
If I didn't want to
touch it, I didn't
have to, I didn't
have to worry, nothing
was going to happen.

Now we were somewhere
among deserted buildings,
back behind a warehouse,
at a loading dock
where the yellow grease-
smeared tongues of
fork lifts stuck out
over the edge above us.
Leaning closer, he said
it's weird, isn't it?,
he said it slowly,
too earnestly,
with so much more fear
than I was feeling
that I began to feel
really afraid.

Then he reached over,
his hand batted my arm
playfully, his fingers
now a language in which
the words make sense
but not sentences,
weirder for being
almost understood.
It's ok, I thought,
this is ok, this one
hand tickling my side,
just like my father's—
("horseplay" my father called it)—
so I squirmed and
giggled, giggled louder
to make it horseplay,

to make myself not
feel the unintelligible
other hand get
my belt unbuckled,
unzip my fly and
with one finger
lift the underwear's
elastic band and let it
snap back, lift and
snap it back again
and again while he only
let himself lean
close enough to peek
in bashfully, peek,
then look away,
as if to show someone
outside the car that
nothing had happened,
see, everything's fine.

A boy is nowhere
else more boy-like
than in the way he
imagines being a man.
My boyhood ended
there, that day, with nothing
else to take its place.
Now I had no name
for what I was.
To try to think it,
say it, was to look
down some vast avenue,

through an infinity
of red lights
and not know any
word for green.

The last day we saw him,
someone's mother was
coming up the street,
coming quickly, yelling
you boys, you
get away, go home,
get away from him.
And he was out of the car,
standing before her
(it was the first time
we'd ever seen him
outside the car),
head bowed, hardly taller
than we were, stammering
I didn't do. . . . I didn't . . .
She'd have him locked up,
did he understand,
locked up with all
the other psychos
if he ever ever
came near her boy again.
Her finger jerking
in his face while
everything about him—
the glassy eyes, the hands
held out in pleading,

and the mouth trembling,
wordless—said back
it wasn't fair, said it
like any boy punished
unfairly, as if her accusation
made him innocent, and this
I would come to think
was what he must have
wanted all along.

At that time, though,
all I saw was the back wheels
of the Sting Ray skidding
as it shrieked away,
the mother stalking after,
still pointing, yelling;
all I could feel
was my throwing hand,
the fingers flexing claw-like
and still more claw-like,
till I got it right.

three

Love Poem

*"If the last day were come, we shouldn't think so
much about the separation of friends or the blighted
prospects of individuals . . . "*

—from *Cape Cod,* Thoreau

Our first warm morning,
and all over the yard
insects had hatched
invisibly and were swarming
up from the grass, innumerable
in a blurred light of wings,
dizzying helixes of rising
through leaf-shadow and sun,
and all so slowly, all
hovering now or dipping
down before they fanned out
higher and wider, as if
to dawdle in that first
moment of their being
suddenly in air, half
resisting their own urge
upward so as to feel
the pull of it more keenly.

Imagine at the appointed hour
what it will be like:
earth's old bonds broken,
all the nations of all time
whirling in a haze, and you
and I lost to each other in that
joyously forgetful going;
imagine our flesh—
the jury-rigged and sweat-stained
ark we danced before,
danced hard as we could
in sun and leaf-shadow—
scoured to mere radiance! Odd,
and not comforting at all,
to think that even to wonder
where you were in that
multitude, to want to
loiter there with you
a little while
among the shadows, would be
too great a gravity
ever to rise against.

Underground

I dreamed it came on
toward us, far away
in the woods where trees,
receding quickly
deeper into trees,
were a fog themselves,
green tufts and grayish
green coils of branch
on branch already
drifting in rough skeins
the fog seemed only
to ravel nearer
now, as if to bear
that dense recession
up to the woods' edge,

and then beyond it,
thicker, through the yard,
and we knew this was
no dream of ours, love,
but a sudden and
irrevocable
waking, underground:

even though we held
our hands out to each
other in that cool
steam, to fend it off,
all we could see was
how the fingers paled
and were gone, and then
the hands, arms, faces;

our eyes the farthest
border it had to
twist through, tangling through
and over till our
every step was still
the same dead center;
the house light's far-off
uncertain aura
still as far away,
and no one calling
Come home now, children,
nobody calling
back to the dissolv-
ing thread our calls were
through that pallid air.

Rock Pool

1

Water roared everywhere around us, yet from the bank
all we could see of it were quick spumes and flashes
here and there, in among the boulders. Cautiously,
as if they might awaken, we clambered over
the gigantic slabs and humps, the sun-baked ovals
lumpy as hammered clay, and saw downstream below us
only the vague shapes of others, almost billowy,
like magnified amoebas, stretching away to even
vaguer ones beyond them, turning the narrow
streambed through the valley to a lunar seam.

2

Easing ourselves down over the massive sides
(we were hot and tired, eager for the pools below)
we could make out older water in the rough grain,
undulating and immobile currents, band swirled on band,
mica-speckled, cloudy, each seeming to move off,
as it faded, through the stone—each one a glacial rune,
each boulder an innumerable pebble in the ice sheet's

tidal suck and drag: two hundred thousand years,
two billion, five, the molten core, spoor
of gasses in the vast night, at our fingertips.

3

Then the pool: your clothes shed, with one hand braced
against the rock ledge you had slipped into the hip-high
rushing water, and were wading out, bent over, reaching
like the blind before you for the slippery boulder
you slid across, pushing against the white weight
of the pouring mist, your skin goose-fleshed, speckled
bright as mica, and then, part mist yourself,
you turned back, smiling, calling though I couldn't
hear you, calling and waving for me to climb down
to where you were, to join you there. And so I did.

Owl

To hear the owl cry
so close to the house
at evening is to think
each time, this time
I'll see it
in some leafless tree.
But the way a switchback
trail dissolves to brush
to reappear briefly
in another direction—
its soft-pitched
four-note wailing seems
drawn out to let me
hear it fall away—
note into note,
into sheer branch
where it's suddenly
in the next tree, more
elusive the closer it comes.

Sometimes half-awakened
in the night I think
it's here, in the room
beside me at my ear,
till I realize it's you,
your voice, dream-molted,
shed of any sense,
or self, and calling up
through dense sleep
only the sound
of its own tracklessness;
so that to put,
as I do, my fingers
lightly to your lips,
to ask, what is it?
what's wrong?
is to be outside
again, and listening,
among the vacant trees.

Guessing Game

It is a child's forest:
the trees all vine sunk,
bole and branch dissolved
to broad-leaved twisted
apparitions rising
over the path, setting
the moss dark air
adrift with shadows
down the darkening slope.

Look how eagerly the couple
goes from turn to
indistinguishable turn,
the suspicion they are lost
so faint, so new to them,
it's still part of the
pleasure of their wandering.

Listen! How small their voices
sound here, rippling away
through large fronds
into denser stillnesses
as each asks the other

now to guess, like children,
where will we be 5 years
from now, or 10?
What will we do there? —

asking as if the future
could be summoned from the
mud-slick nubs
of stone they help each
other over; as if the path
in its vague forks and jags
opened for them alone.

But there are children
wandering through the lovers'
voices: the little boy
and girl of an old tale,
hand in hand, go with them
guessing through the shadows;

still lost, still parentless
but able to be brave,
their faces brave still,
as in the pictures,
because father is coming!

Listen! Can't you hear him
up ahead? Can't you
hear his big step
hurrying to meet us?

Marriage

When she saw him in the mirror watching,
she said, honey, don't you know that marriage
means the end of voyeurism—this sort at least?
Hip out, on tiptoe, she had twisted
her naked torso back toward the mirror
and with her right hand lifted
the cheek up gingerly so she could see
the insect bite high on the thigh.
What other sort was there?

                            But she just
laughed in answer, laughed sadly,
so it seemed, the way you laugh at
some incorrigibly foolish longing—
her own? his?—as if she'd long since
given up expecting him to see more
than what the mirror showed him then
as she returned to the examination,
as if he wasn't there, and she
weren't his, not yet: desire by any
ruse still clinging to the new,
lingering at the threshold—always
to feel, to be there on the verge

of crossing over, breathlessly . . .
What he saw now in the mirror
was not the smooth torque of the stomach,
the fine breast-shaded ripple
of the ribs. But what she held from him.

Seventh Month

Even her hands seem hardly hers now.
In the full-length mirror she watches
their slow shy clock- and counterclockwise
motion on the spine-slung globe of belly.
Like a conversation in another room,
words muffled to a senseless melody,
the circles within circles which her fingers
trace over the tender sheen, the downy
ligature of skin, are somehow calls
to what whirls soundlessly beyond her fingers,
calls and counter-calls too intimate
to be perceived as anything but
looping touch, feathery roll and kick,
herself half host, half reluctant
interloper to these private greetings.

In her nightly dream, she's thirsty,
looking down into the black shaft of a well,
the stone she drops in falls and falls,
and when she hurls herself down
what terrifies her is the wild glee,
the quenching weightlessness. She says
these days she wants to go on all fours
like a dog. It wouldn't ache so much.
She says, this must be what the way
I looked before had wanted. She turns
sideways and says, oh god, where am I?

Tour for Expecting Parents

Someone had scribbled *Celebrate* on a pink balloon
and tied it to the incubator nearest the window,
in a room of incubators. The baby froglike
on its stomach, a scraggly vine of tubes and wires
all over its back. More than two months premature,
the nurse said, the small face hardly a face,
crumpled like a wad of balled-up paper, the eyes
mere creases, the lips thread-thin, quivering;
but what I couldn't take my eyes from was the purple
cilia of toes and fingers twitching, trying to twitch,
as if even the air weighed against them too heavy to lift.
As nurses hurried coolly around the incubator
batting the balloon by accident with shoulder or elbow,
          the word swayed cheerfully.

What scared me then was not that I could see
my soon to be born child in that child's place,
but that I somehow wanted to see it there, to feel
my eagerness turn, as it did, to an old fear
so familiar it was almost comforting.
I saw that it's for no one's sake but mine,
this too eager habit of anticipating trouble,
as if worry alone meant love, and not a loveless

privacy in camouflage, desiring
not to feel at all, to hide by thinking
if I never let myself forget I'm at the mercy
of what I can't help, I could then be
less the victim of it. What that child needed,
        though, was a harder

readiness for joy that's no less ready
despite remembering it can never be
its own good luck, that the unforeseen
and unforeseeable is, no matter what we do,
already flying toward us out of everywhere
to strike the love we'll soon lift like a target.
To see that someone knew this and could still
scrawl that one word, *Celebrate,* above the child,
was to see what I have never done
and didn't know even now if I could do,
watching that one word float above the child,
above the child like a signal back and forth
before me, like a warning now, or promise,
        now like a plea.

In the Kingdom of Pleasure

Unwitting accomplice in the scheme of law
she thought to violate, man-set as it was,
and, here, inconsequential as the sun
at midnight, drought at flood-time—
when she heard a baby in the tall reeds
at the river's brink, she was nobody's
daughter, subject of no rule
but the one his need for her established
as she knelt down to quell his crying
with a little tune just seeing him there
had taught her how to hum.

                                Now as then,
it is the same tune, timelessly in time,
your mother hums as she kneels down
beside your little barge of foam,
smiling to see you smile when she wrings
out from the sponge a ragged string
of water over the chest and belly,
the dimpled loins, the bud so far
from flowering, and the foot slick

as a fish your hand tries to hold up
till it slips back splashing
with such mild turbulence that she laughs,
and you laugh to see her laugh.

Here now, as it was then, it is still
so many years before the blood's smeared
over doorposts, before the Nile clots
with the first-born, and the women
wailing, wailing throughout the city;
here now again is the kingdom of pleasure,
where they are safe still, mother and child,
from the chartered rod of the Fathers,
and where a father can still pray, Lord,
Jealous Chooser, Devouring Law, keep
away from them, just keep away.

Separation of the Waters

*"When God commanded, 'Let the waters be
gathered together, unto one place, and let the dry
land appear,' certain parts refused to obey. They
embraced each other all the more closely."*

—Jewish Legend

In his voice I hear the first day
        of the waters,
before the spirit moved, brooding,
        over the face of them,

before the firmament appearing
        in the wake of His Word
divided upper water from lower water,
        heaven from earth,

on the second day. Here in his voice
        the first day
once again refuses the command
        to be the second,

vowel and phoneme all awash, inchoate
        in a jubilant babble
I lean over the crib to watch, that goes on
        after he sees me,

after I say the name he hears as nonsense
        the way the waters heard,
so entangled in the waters, whelmed
        in the jubilant eddy

of such complete embracing they couldn't
        have known themselves
as water, when the Lord said,
        "Let the waters part."

See how as on the shore of speech, lonely
        for him, I call and call.
See how the syllables begin to dampen,
        blur and dissolve back,

close as they can now, toward the far surf
        they were torn from,
from the shore of the sixth day calling
        back to the first.

Dawn Chorus

When the gate swung shut
behind you, did you
hear these songs? these same
small trills and mingled
half-chimes through the heart
of Eden, running
away so shyly,
in new and ever
newer syllables
that must have seemed then
to your outcast ears
no less delighted

for your being gone?
Is it you in us
they hide from? And are
we, then, as we look
up into bright leaves
seamless as a flame,

furtive with such sheer
singing, are we there,
again, where you stood,
still at the threshold
of the lush unknowing
you had forfeited?

Kinship

At the sound the dog was one hard nerve of attention
to the moon-pleated shadows of the woods at the road's edge;
his hackles blade-like, tail erect; stiller, it seemed,
with each stride of what was moving near us, like leaves
rustling over leaves, neither farther away nor closer,
and prowling back and forth in the same place as if held there
hesitant and slow before the breathing wall we were.
The dog sprang in the moment it leaped away.

I could hear them tangled together in their running
through the rough brush, in and out of gullies, down
the dark leads of the sloping woods: that powerful
long bounding and the frantic harrying behind it
merged as they faded to a drumbeat, heartbeat.
And though I called and called, my voice tapered
to nothing in the gathered shadows, and I could not
remember kneeling to take up the stone my hand now held.

Turkey Vultures

Always at evening they glide in, thirty or more,
like a gathering night chaff high over the woods
behind the house, their long wings barely swaying,
banking as they wheel over us till one by one they loop down
into the crabbed maze of the same (always the same)
tall oaks, where the wings now suddenly flared
rustle heavily against the branches as they settle.

Hard not to think of them as waiting, they are so still—
bunched three or four together still as moss, black moss
in the crook of branches, and others alone out at the ends
like fruit weighing them down. It is hard not to think
the gray gauze of the trees behind them, reddish leaf mold
and pale fungus on the ground, and even the house itself—

porch, wood frame, sills and floors—are darkened by them,
quickened with their dark, and that soon they will be
the single watching of the night perched all around us
as we go from room to room, to draw the curtains,
seeing the same wing flutter up and hover
over every light that flickers to go on.

Prayer on the Temple Steps

Devious guide, strange parent,
what are you
but the movable ways
I lose you by?
Opulent honeycomb
of nowhere
where the bee-ghosts cluster,
hymning your each cell
with all the sweetness that you hold
from me,
    so I might know
instead the fitful aspic
of this readiness—
      what is it
you bring out of the veils
of air but this, these words—
gate opening on to you
and burning sword
above it turning
every way I turn.

T u r n

Speech is the candle here—see the dark made mobile
now about its tongue, the gathering dark of voices
earlier than ours, and others still earlier, voice
ringed on voice out to the first rough filial hue and cry.
Here, we say, I'm here, turn to me now. Who is it speaking
in the circling namelessness? By whose breath is the flame fanned?
Speech is the candle I hold up to see you
and the night bent down to cup us in its giant hand.

four

Home Movie

—for Beth and Russ

That's your father, she tells us, when he was nice.
Our father with you sleeping in his arms, his first-born,
his month-old daughter, and our mother next to him—
when I was pretty, wasn't I pretty?—her blond hair
banged and glossy, and her bright face keen above
the clean white petals of her blouse's collar,
keen and yet stiff too, smiling for the camera
at the baby she just knows she'll be a sister to,
and at the husband who could be a movie star,
he's such a looker, then out at us, forty years away,
then back again, the whole time smiling, smiling,
eager to seem as happy as she is. She's just nineteen.
Impossible to tell, meanwhile, which part is love
and which part shyness keeps him staring down
at you and never at the camera, his big hand
fussing the blanket back below your chin,
even after she starts teasing, elbowing his side
to make her "big baby" smile, just once, at us.
Yet there's something sure there too, skilled even,
in the clumsily tender way he holds you out now
like a thing too precious to be held, as if

he knew it made him better-looking, that furtive
half smile harder to resist because withheld so long,
taken back so quickly, which is why he's not surprised
when she laughs at this and kisses him on the cheek;
no, not surprised but boyishly triumphant—to have
won over, so easily, so beautiful a woman.

Their good looks float unsteadily on the scored surface.
Hard, and long, and unimaginable—the way here.
Imagine, though, we were the movie they were watching,
and they knew us, knew who we were, as in a dream,
a bad dream he would not believe—your husband's black skin
like a cruel prank and, crueler, your lighter daughter
sleeping in your lap, your first-born, late child
we have come to celebrate, and, no, that couldn't be
his wife beside you, overweight, sad, everything
inscrutable but her sadness, which he'd misunderstand;
and she, too, still a child herself, like any child
would be afraid what her friends would say, her family,
baffled to be in the picture, baffled yet maybe
reassured as well, her hopes not entirely unfounded,
to see how eagerly she lifts the baby out of your arms
because you're tired and should go lie down, and how
you two laugh together, as if you'd done so always,
when she takes the tiny fingers in her finger
and waves them forty years away to where
she's waving your hand in the same finger.
Bitter, and long, and unforeseeable—what changes,
what survives! She holds the small hand toward us
and in a girl's voice, wonderstruck, says she read
somewhere how the skin will darken as the child gets older:
Isn't it lovely how dark it is under the fingernail?

Two Elegies

1. Irma

"It's Irma, just calling
to see how everybody is . . . "
your voice caught

in the static of the old tape
faint, half-erased,
yet cheerful as ever,

so for a moment
it was easy to believe
you had called that day.

It would have been just
like you—never to betray
the slightest disappointment,

even to seem relieved
we weren't in,
your cheerfulness unchallenged,

no one to coax from you
what day by day
was harder to keep hidden:

bad eyes, bad heart,
the body now so
erratic with need

your dignity contracted to these
fixed amenities.
It would have been

just like you—
when you arrived
among the tongueless dead—

to call us, to have us hear
in the firm voice
firmer for the static,

how calmly
you preempt our pity
by asking how everybody is.

2. Dotty

In the only photograph
I have of you, I'm raw
exuberance, all nerves
and angles, breathless,
losing my way

within the labyrinth
of turn and half-turn,
cha, cha, and kick
while you glide freely.
Since it's my wedding night,
you have taken up my left hand so
tactfully in your right
that as you twirl beneath it
anyone who sees us
has to think, as I do,
that I'm leading.

I can see too, now,
years later, how your full smile
cagey with gratitude
has fooled me into feeling
that my motion doesn't merely
match the gracefulness of yours
but makes it possible.

Hiding me as best you can
from my wild left-footedness,
you seem to say,
let him have this night,
let this one night be his.
You seem to know
that I would see you
there, enisled
in the first hard month
after your husband's death,
just months before
your cancer's diagnosed;

you smiling graciously,
graciously and (I know now)
not without a little
condescension as I move,
as from my own beginnings,
toward you, as you lead me on.

Purgatory

They are there now on the twilit platform,
all of them glancing at each other
in a tightly strung decorum
it confuses them to know so well.
Like a sleep they can't quite
yield to, or shake,
everything they see—
the broken heating lamp,
the trash bin, benches—
is veiled in a wavering air
of unplaceable reminders.

All they can think to say
are tag ends of phrases,
debris of idioms they repeat
and shrug at helplessly—
Far Out . . . I wouldn't give
two cents . . . My luck . . .

How odd, too, still to be shifting,
steadying bundles in their arms
for ease, when they're not tired;
still to be stamping their feet,
beating thick-coated arms, breath
steamy, when they aren't cold.
Why must they lean out
over the edge to watch the rails
curve into far-off trees; why want
to see the rails flare, the flare
slide nearer, the train light glimmer
through the branches till it
floats free, drawing the train behind?

It's as if these gestures
were a rumor of some missed
connection that concerns them,
a map they still know
how to follow even after
they've forgotten what a map is.

If we would only think of them
a young girl might come
skipping up the stairs,
vain, foolish, smiling at
no one, humming some silly tune
that's her own affair—
yet they would see her
rising toward them like a flower
from the lower dark

and in the light of her
would know the words
for uncle, friend,
lover, child and parent;
with their own names
suddenly sayable
they would see, beyond,
in answer to her coming,
how the light glides free
of the branches
down the black trough,
closer; just as in answer,
too, they would feel
again the glad weight
of these belongings
heavier in their grasp
as they are drawn now
to the girl, to swarm
around her, gently,
unhurriedly,
certain that where she is
is where the doors will open.

Memory, Memory,
see how they wait there
in the mere occasion
of their looking
everywhere around—
see how they wait for you,
too shy to ask
(even if they knew how),
Is this the right stop?
Am I supposed to be here?

Covenant

The oldest sister, her two hands on the table,
about to push herself up, stares with grim
determination at the affronting dishes,
waiting, it seems, until the middle sister
finishes her story, so she can clear them away.
Her gaze so tense with purpose she can almost
see germs spawning in the mess of white fish
flaking from the spines, the smear of egg yolk
and the torn rolls disfiguring the china;
as if the meal, the moment it is over,
the meal she made a point of telling them
she shopped for, got up early to prepare,
were now inedible, because uneaten.
It's no great comfort either that her brother
sitting opposite holds up a flared match
over the pipe from which smoke rolls away
across the table like a phantom mold
in and around the open tub of butter,
the gouged block of cream cheese and the coffee cups;
so in a moment when she finally does stand

she'll say again, as always, For love or money
in my mouth I'd never put such filth,
and he'll say, winking at the middle sister,
That's what she said on her honeymoon.

The youngest sister is sitting on the couch
behind the table; her face—sheer disengagement,
toneless and still—appears to hang suspended
beyond the oldest sister's shoulder, far
enough away for no one yet to notice
as her legs cross that the ashtray in her lap
spills ash over the sunflowers of her housedress.
Or that the cigarette between her fingers
sags loosely and is dangling while the hand
lifts like a puppet's on a string of smoke.

Her death is just three months away.

Even though it's summer (otherwise
the brother and middle sister would be home,
in Florida), summer and late morning—
with sunlight only just now catching on
a corner of the window shut behind them,
shut against the smog, the steady traffic
and the panicked blare and drawn-out whining fade
of sirens—the apartment is still quiet,
still cool enough, right now, to keep the body
in the wavering frail zone of what it needs
to be forgotten, so they can sit like this
together, with the oldest sister's sharp eye
on the wrecked meal, the brother and sister talking:

Listen, she would be saying, listen, Charlie,
her elbows on the table, both hands open,
the body fashioned to the voice's weary
What can you do? What are ya gonna do?
in answer to some story of a cousin's
sudden illness (And he was my age, just
like that one day he's shaving with the toothpaste),
or a friend's death (That one, she didn't care
how sick she got, she always had her hair done),
his back pain, her arthritis, or the daughter
who won't diet (And she'd be such a beauty!);
after his joke about the nurse, and hers
about the bedpan, Listen, they each say,
Listen, what are ya gonna do?

                        "The Schmo,
he never should've married her, for Christ sake,
until he told her that he had a problem,
that was his first mistake, then he goes
throwing away his pills, because he's happy
he doesn't need them anymore, the schmo,
so of course what happens is she wakes up
and finds him weeping at the kitchen table,
just weeping, he doesn't know why, he won't eat,
won't get dressed, says he's quittin' his job,
you know, nuts, nuts, so naturally she leaves him,
the poor schmo, and he's such a good boy . . . "

All of the harm that's imperceptibly
but surely coming for them (the way the sun
burns brick by brick all morning toward the window
like a slow fuse)—all of the bad news now
is in the body only enough to hold
the middle sister's two hands open, shrug

her shoulders in a way they recognize
as hers, the way their mother did; as if
all trouble were, for now, no heavier
than the familiar voice repeating, Listen,
Listen it could be worse; So who's to say?;
What was, was; When your number's up—like old charms
woven around each story till they've made
what happens what was only meant to happen,
coherent with fate, fated as family.

After the funeral three months from now,
they'll have to listen to the oldest sister
tell them they had no business moving away
to Florida, and Irene sick as she was.
And selfish. She was selfish, that one. After
all those years of living with that bum,
her husband, may his cheap soul rest in peace,
didn't *she* deserve a little pleasure?
And anyway, what could be done for her?
Didn't the stroke just make it easier
for her to sit all day, and smoke, and not care
ashes were falling on the couch, the carpet;
her bathrobe filthy, filthy? Oh it was terrible—
and now they will hear the old unfairnesses,
old feuds and resentments come to her voice
like consolation, like a mother helping
her recite the story of that last bad day—
all that smoke, and running in with nothing
but the dishtowel to beat down the flames,
and Irene, just Irene, just sitting there,
the queen of Sheba—What difference did it make
since *she* was there, *she* was always there,
her big sister, to clean up the mess?

Only three months, and yet it could be years,
or decades, for the sun has only just now
caught in the window, and its bright plaque warms
the air so gradually that none of them
can know it's warming, or that soon someone,
distracted by a faint sheen prickling the skin,
will break the story, look up toward the window
and, startled by the full glare, check the time.
Right now, though, the future is a luxury
of instances in which the cigarette,
raised halfway to the lips, will go on rising.
Nothing bad, right now, can happen here
except as news, bad news the brother and sister
mull and rehearse, puzzle and fret until
it seems the very telling of it is
what keeps them safe. And safe, too, the oldest sister,
dreaming of all the perishables sealed,
wrapped up and hurried back into the fridge's
uncontaminated airlessness,
dreaming of how the soapsuds curdle and slide
over the dishes in a soothing fury,
not minding that it scalds her hands to hold
each plate and cup and bowl under the hot,
hard jet of water, if it gets them clean.